Looking after your
HAMSTER

**A Young Pet Owner's Guide
by Helen Piers**

FRANCES LINCOLN

Text and illustrations copyright © Helen Piers 1992, 2002

First published in Great Britain in 1992
by Frances Lincoln Limited
ISBN 0-7112-0709-7

This revised edition is first published in Great Britain in 2002
by Frances Lincoln Limited, 4 Torriano Mews,
Torriano Avenue, London NW5 2RZ

www.franceslincoln.com

The author and publishers would like to thank the children who were
photographed with their hamsters for this book, Sarah Meynink BVSc, MRCVS,
of the Ark Veterinary Clinics, London SW6, and Petsville of Kingston-upon-Thames,
Surrey, for their help. Special thanks are due to Iain Bownes BVSc, MRCVS,
of the Grange Veterinary Clinic, Bermondsey, London SE1 and Anne Wignall,
formally of the RSPCA, Horsham, Sussex, for their professional advice.
The RSPCA has approved this text.

The author and publishers would also like to thank Marion Hawkes,
B.Vet Med, MRCVS, of Old Courts Veterinary Centre in Brigg for checking
and updating this revised edition.

British Library Cataloguing in Publication Data
available on request.

ISBN 0-7112-1926-5

Printed and bound in Hong Kong

9 8 7 6 5 4 3 2 1

Contents

Hamsters as pets

A fully grown hamster is about 10 cm long. It is mouse-like in shape, but plumper and sturdier. Its fur is soft and silky, and it has almost no tail.

Once tame, a hamster will let itself be handled and stroked without fear.

If you have never kept a pet before, a hamster is one of the best with which to start. Hamsters are gentle and good-tempered, and when handled kindly and patiently soon lose any fear of people, and become very tame.

If you decide to keep a hamster, you will need to buy or make a cage for it, but after that it will cost very little to feed and look after. Its cage will be easy to clean, and it will not take up much space.

Some people think that hamsters are not such good pets because they sleep most of the day, and are awake and busy at night when everybody else wants to sleep. But if a hamster is taken out and played with at the same time every evening or late afternoon, it will look forward to this, and begin to wake up earlier.

The hamsters kept as pets are usually *Golden* hamsters. This species was thought extinct. Then in 1930 a female and her litter of babies was found in the Syrian desert, and taken to Europe. Every pet Golden hamster today is descended from this one family.

Golden hamsters were originally all golden brown with creamy white on the underside of the body, the eyes large and black, and the ears grey or black. But now there are many other colour varieties as well.

You can find white hamsters, cream, grey and all shades of brown, some the same colour all over, others banded or patterned in two or more colours. Some have red or ruby eyes instead of black.

Their coats can vary too. The short velvety coated hamsters are called *satins*. There are also long-haired fluffy ones.

NOTE: If you want to keep *Russian* hamsters read page 30, because they do need looking after a little differently.

5

Understanding hamsters

A hamster needs a nesting box where it can hide away and feel as safe as it would in its burrow under the ground.

To understand your hamster better, you need to know a little about how it would live if it were wild.

Golden hamsters come from hot desert lands, where they burrow under the ground to shelter from the heat of the sun during the daytime, and only come out to look for their food when it is cool in the evening. That is why your hamster sleeps during the day, and is awake and busy at night.

Food is hard to find in the desert. A wild hamster would travel far from its burrow, searching in the sand for seeds and the occasional green plant. Your pet hamster does not have to forage for its food but it still needs a lot of exercise. So it must have room in its cage to move about freely, an exercise wheel to run in, and perhaps a ladder to climb up and down.

During one night a hamster may travel as much as a mile or two just running in its wheel.

Wild hamsters hoard food when it is plentiful, in case of a shortage later. Hamsters have special cheek pouches into which they can stuff food and carry it back to a store in their burrow.

The instinct to hoard is still strong in a pet hamster. So, although you will be there to feed it regularly, your hamster will also use its cheek pouches and store food behind its nest.

Golden hamsters are solitary – each one living alone in its own burrow, which it defends fiercely. That is why hamsters must be caged singly, or they will fight for ownership of the cage.

A hamster's cheek pouches can hold food weighing half as much as itself.

Hamsters are rodents – animals which 'gnaw'. Like other rodents, a hamster's teeth go on growing all its life. It must be given something hard to gnaw on and wear them down, or they will grow so long it can no longer eat.

Things you will need

Checklist

- cage
- nesting box
- exercise wheel
- sawdust
- nesting materials:
    hay
        white paper
        cotton rags
        cardboard
- food dishes
- drip-feed water bottle
- food
    packet hamster mix
    vegetables
- small branch or piece of hardwood for gnawing on

A nesting box

Sawdust for the floor of the cage

A block or a small branch of hardwood

Food (see checklist)

One kind of hamster cage (there are others over the page)

A drip-feed water bottle is better than a bowl for water, as it keeps the water clean.

Heavy earthenware dishes are best, because they do not get knocked over easily.

An exercise wheel: do not get one made of metal bars, in which the hamster might catch its foot.

Nesting materials
(see also checklist and NEVER box)

Never

On the cage floor
Never use wood wool – the hamster may get tangled in its long strands.
Nesting materials
Never give newspaper – printing ink is poisonous. *Never* cotton wool, knitting wool, or man-made fibres – they can cause a blockage in a hamster's stomach. And *never* straw – it scratches the inside of the hamster's cheek pouches.
Wood for gnawing
Never give laburnum or evergreen wood – they are poisonous. *Never* softwood – it splinters easily. *Never* put anything made of thin plastic in the cage – if the hamster swallows bits, it cannot digest them.

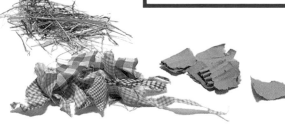

The cage

Remember

- Will the cage allow your hamster to take all the exercise it needs?
- Is it escape-proof?
- Is it safe from other pets?
- Is it well-ventilated?
- Is there a place in it where the hamster can build its nest and feel safe and private?

Pet shops stock various kinds of cage, or you may want to build your own. Your hamster is going to spend all its life in the cage you provide for it, so choose carefully.

How big should the cage be?
An average cage is about 48 x 24 x 24 cm. But the bigger the better. The ideal size would be 75 x 40 x 40 cm.

Will the cage allow your hamster to take all the exercise it needs?
Hamsters are very active. They need to run, climb and burrow. A smaller cage which has a shelf with a ladder up to it can be as good for the hamster and more interesting than a larger one in which it can run about on one level only. Most cages include an exercise wheel. If not, you can buy one separately.

This home-made cage has been built of 8mm plywood lined with formica. Joins are made with glue and panel pins. The whole front slides open sideways and is made of rigid wire mesh so that enough air can get into the cage.

Instead of having a door, the whole top lifts off this cage, which is very useful when you are feeding or taming your hamster.

Is the cage escape-proof?

Hamsters are good at escaping. They can gnaw through soft wood and squeeze through narrow gaps. Be especially careful about this if you make your own cage.

Will your hamster be sheltered enough?

Your hamster will be more sheltered in a cage with a solid back and sides. However, these cages are not easy to find ready-made, so if your cage has bars all round, keep it tucked into a corner, out of draughts.

Nesting boxes

Your hamster will need a nesting box. You can buy one or make one out of hardwood. It should have a lid so that you can easily check whether your hamster is storing mouldy food.

Try to buy your hamster in the afternoon when they are more lively. In the morning most of them will be sleepy. At the pet shop several hamsters may be kept together. This is possible because they are still very young.

It is important to choose a healthy hamster. Ask if you can look at the one you choose outside its cage.

Buying a hamster

Your pet shop will probably have a number of hamsters in stock, and you should take time choosing the one you like best.

What age should the hamster be?
It is best to buy your hamster when it is between four and seven weeks old, because it will be easier to tame when young.

Does it matter which sex the hamster is?
Male and female hamsters are equally good-tempered and easy to tame. But remember you can never keep two hamsters in one cage, because they will fight.

How to tell if a hamster is healthy
Its body should be smooth and well-rounded, not bony.

Its coat should be clean, particularly on the underside of the body, with no bare patches.

Its ears should be clean inside, and, if it is young, covered with hair outside.

Its eyes should be bright and clean, not runny.

There should be no pimples on ears, nose, feet or belly.

What food is the hamster used to?
Ask what food it has been eating, so you can give the same. If you want to feed it differently, wait a week or so, and then change to other foods gradually.

The pet shop will give you a cardboard box in which to take your hamster home. But if your journey lasts longer than two hours it may nibble a way out. So take along a small wooden or plastic box. It must fasten securely and have air holes. Put hay and a little food in the bottom.

Taking the hamster home

If you have made your own cage, or bought one earlier, you can get it ready before you go out to buy your hamster.

Your hamster may be nervous after the journey, so instead of picking it up to put in the cage, place its carrying box open on the floor of the cage, and let it come out to explore when it is ready.

When you reach home, settle your hamster into its cage as soon as possible.

Wash out the cage with a few drops of mild disinfectant in the water.

Rinse and dry it well.

Cover the cage floor with a deep layer of sawdust and throw in a small heap of nesting material – hay, white paper, cotton material and cardboard. Put a little in the nesting box to encourage your hamster to make its nest there.

Lastly, put some food in the cage and fix up the drip-feed water bottle. Put in the gnawing wood, the exercise wheel and perhaps a cardboard roller for your hamster to play in.

It is not wise to play with your hamster straight away. The journey could have been stressful for it, so leave it alone and quiet to explore its new home.

Where should the cage be kept?

Keep the cage indoors – it will be too cold outside. But never put it close to a window which gets hot afternoon sun, or by a radiator, or in a draught.

Remember to put the cage out of reach of cats. Although a cat cannot get in, it could frighten your hamster by trying to put its paw between the bars, or by sitting watching beside the cage, or even on top of it!

You will know your hamster is settling down happily in its new home when you see it beginning to make its nest or run in its wheel.

Feeding 1

Hamsters eat seeds, grains and nuts, vegetables, and a little fruit.

Hamster mix

Hamster mix is sold in pet shops. It is specially prepared to provide a hamster with a well-balanced diet of its essential foods – grains, seeds and nuts.

Vegetables

Both root and green vegetables should be given, always raw.

Give fresh water every day

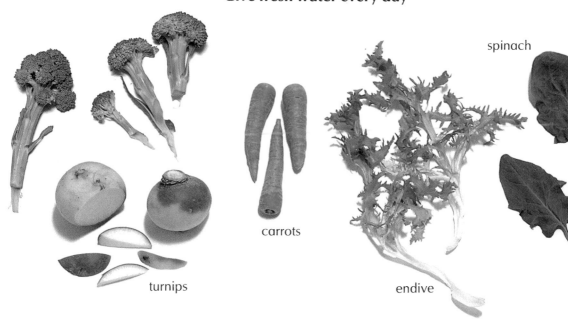

spinach

carrots

turnips

endive

Some vegetables which are very good for your hamster

16

How often should a hamster be fed?

Feed your hamster once a day, in the late afternoon or evening.

How much food does it need?

Give a small handful of hamster mix and a small handful of vegetables. If any is left uneaten, give less next day. If all is eaten, try giving more, but first check your hamster is not hoarding it in its store!

> ### *Remember*
>
> - Feed at the same time every day.
> - Wash fruit and vegetables well.
> - Give raw, fresh vegetables – never cooked or frozen.
> - Give a good variety of foods, but introduce any new food gradually.

parsley

> After your hamster is 12 weeks old, you can give *small amounts* of cabbage, Brussels sprouts and lettuce – but *not* Iceberg lettuce.

outside leaves and stalk of cauliflower

(More about feeding over page.)

Feeding 2

Extra vitamins

To make sure your hamster gets the vitamins it needs, you can buy vitamin drops for small animals at the pet shop.

Water

Never leave your hamster without fresh water to drink. It is wrong to think it can go without because it is a desert animal. In the desert hamsters drink the morning dew and find water in water-storing plants.

As occasional treats hamsters enjoy sultanas, fruit cake, dog biscuits, sunflower seeds and chopped hard-boiled egg. But be careful – too many sunflower seeds can cause skin troubles.

Fruit

You can feed pieces of apple, pear, grape and tomato, all in small amounts only. But fruit goes off quickly, and if your hamster eats bad fruit it will be ill. So check none is left uneaten in the cage or food store for more than a day.

When you want to go on holiday

If you are going away, you should take your hamster with you, or arrange for a friend to feed it. Your hamster will need a daily check, to ensure it is well, and has enough food and clean water.

Wild plants

If you can recognise them, you can give dandelion, shepherd's purse, yarrow, chickweed, clover and groundsel leaves, and also young raspberry leaves (no prickly stalks). *But be careful! Many wild plants are poisonous.*

Never

Never give your hamster salted nuts, crisps, chocolate, sweets or anything sticky, which could get lodged in its cheek pouches.
Never gather wild plants from beside a road, because of pollution, and *never* from a lawn sprayed with insecticides.

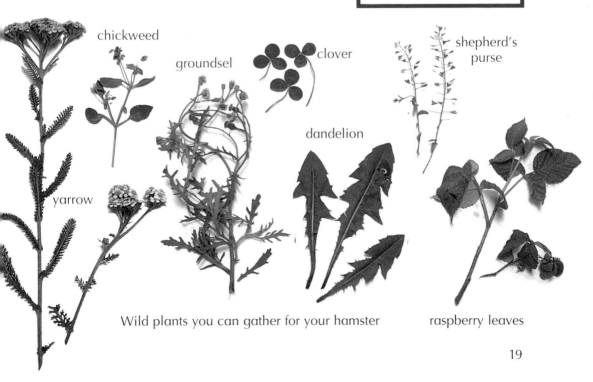

chickweed

groundsel

clover

shepherd's purse

dandelion

yarrow

Wild plants you can gather for your hamster

raspberry leaves

19

Taming and handling

Before you handle your hamster you will need to tame it, which means overcoming its fear. You will enjoy doing this as long as you understand it will take time and patience. Do not put it off, because it will be easier while your hamster is still young.

Talk to your hamster all the time you are taming it. It will get to know your voice. Move your hands gently – they must seem large and frightening to a small animal.

You should be able to tame your hamster in less than three weeks, if you follow the method opposite. Do not rush it, or you may have to start all over again.

Do hamsters bite?

Only if they are frightened. A nip from a young hamster is not really painful, and not harmful. If your hamster does nip your finger, try not to frighten it more by jerking your hand away or screaming.

Never

Never wake your hamster if it is sleeping deeply.
Never shout or make sudden jerky movements.
Never pick up a hamster from behind – let it see your hand.
Never grip it tightly – let it run from one hand to the other.

Remember

- Play with your hamster at the same time every day.
- Speak to it softly all the time.
- Play with it for short times only, but often.
- Handle it over a table or near the ground, so that if you drop it, it does not have far to fall.

1 First watch your hamster for a few days to find out when it is awake and active – the best time to start taming. Note its favourite foods so you can use them to overcome its fear.

    Now start putting food straight on the cage floor, so your hamster gets used to your hand and learns that it brings food and means no harm. After a few days, leave your hand there while the hamster eats.

2 When your hamster is confident enough to eat beside your hand, put the food in the palm of your hand. It may be some time before the hamster will eat from your hand without fear. When it does, you can stroke it gently with one finger along its back, the way the fur grows. *Never* stroke its head.

3 Next, get your hamster used to being picked up. When it is eating from your hand, cup the other hand over it, and lift it gently a little way off the ground for a few moments at a time.

    After a few more days, if your hamster seems happy being lifted up, you can take it right out of the cage in your cupped hands.

4 Play with it over a table, letting it run from one hand to the other. Soon it will be confident enough to run along your arm.

Exercise and play

Do not leave your hamster alone when it is out of its cage. You never know what it may get up to. Some hamsters will climb anything, and hide in quite unexpected places!

If you keep the hamster cage in your bedroom you will soon find out how busy your hamster is at night, digging in the sawdust and running in its wheel.

But for such an active animal, exercising inside its cage is not enough, and hamsters enjoy a daily playtime out of the cage.

An escape-proof play-space can be made from hardboard or a large wooden crate with sides about 30 cm high, and sawdust in the bottom (for digging in).

Your hamster may be nervous at first and run to the nearest hiding place. But have it out every day, and it will soon grow confident.

You can put branches, boxes, cardboard tubes, flower pots, and other things in the play-space to make it more interesting for your hamster.

If you decide to give your hamster the run of the room, first make sure it is escape-proof. There may be gaps between floor boards or under doors, which you never noticed before, but which your hamster will find at once. These must be blocked up.

Also make sure there is no electric wiring for your hamster to nibble and get a shock. And remember to check on the cat!

It is better not to give your hamster the run of the room until it is tame.

Having your hamster out to play before it is tame

If your hamster is not yet tame enough to be picked up, put a small cardboard box on the cage floor. When your hamster runs into it, you can carry the box with the hamster inside to the play-space.

Capturing a lost hamster

Try putting food in the cage, and leave it with the door open near where you think the hamster is hiding. During the night when it is hungry it will probably return and you will find it curled up in its nest in the morning.

Another way of recapturing a lost hamster is to make a ramp with a piece of wood up to a bucket, in which you have put some food. When it is hungry the hamster will run up the ramp and jump down into the bucket to get the food. It will not be able to climb out until you come for it.

Cleaning and grooming

If your hamster is to stay healthy, its cage must be kept clean, and never allowed to become damp.

Once a day
Take away left-over food, remove any wet sawdust, and replace with fresh.

Once a week
Sweep out all sawdust and replace with fresh. Do not disturb the nest or food store except to remove any food which is going bad.

Once a month
Clear out the whole cage, and nesting box. Wash it in soapy water with a few drops of mild disinfectant added. *Rinse and dry well* before putting in fresh sawdust and nesting material.

Cleaning out the cage is not an unpleasant job if you do it often enough.

The nest and food store

Some hamsters get upset when these are removed. So perhaps when you clear out the nest, you could put back a little of the old nesting material to make it smell right. Then your hamster will not be too unhappy.

Long-haired hamsters need regular grooming to keep their coats in good condition. Use a soft toothbrush and be very gentle. Your hamster should enjoy it.

Hamsters are very flexible, and when they groom themselves they reach every part of their bodies.

Grooming

A short-haired hamster will groom itself very well. If it gets very dirty, perhaps after hiding in some dusty corner, it can be brushed gently with a soft toothbrush. When really necessary, dampen the brush with warm water, but never let your hamster get too wet.

Health

If you think your hamster may be ill, do not put off taking it to a vet. The vet will know if anything serious is the matter, and what to do about it.

A hamster is usually healthy if it is fed correctly and given enough exercise, and its cage is kept clean, dry, and out of draughts. But even the best cared-for hamsters sometimes get ill.

How do you know when a hamster is ill?
It may refuse to eat.
It may sit huddled up, tired and sleepy.
It may have dirty, wet fur around its tail – a sign of diarrhoea.
Its eyes or its nose may be runny.
Its fur may be dull.
There may be bare patches in its fur.

What to do if your hamster seems ill
If you are at all worried, take your hamster to your veterinary surgeon. Meanwhile make sure your hamster is warm and has plenty of fresh water.

On the next page are some of the more common illnesses and their symptoms.

Ask the vet to look at your hamster's teeth. A hamster's teeth go on growing all its life. If not worn down by constant gnawing, they may grow so long that it cannot eat.

Symptoms	Possible cause and what to do
Sneezing, sore eyes and runny nose	This may be an *allergy*, perhaps to some nesting material, air freshener, or spray polish. But it could be a *cold*, so keep your hamster warm, and if no better next day, **take it to the vet**.
Fur around the tail very dirty, and possibly wet	Your hamster has *diarrhoea*, perhaps caused only by eating something which did not agree with it. But this could be the first sign of a serious illness called *wet tail*, so **take your hamster to the vet at once**.
Bare patches in the fur	This may be just old age, or the hamster may have rubbed itself against something and worn the fur away. But if it is scratching the bare patches, they could be caused by *mites*. The vet will give you something to clear them up.
Refusal to eat, a swollen cheek, and runny eyes	Your hamster has something stuck in its cheek pouch. **Take it to the vet**.
After a fall, or being handled too much, the hamster lies quite still, as if dead	It is in a state of shock, though it may not be seriously hurt. If you leave it in a quiet, warm place, it should recover in an hour or two. **If not, take it to the vet.**
Cuts – the hamster has cut itself on something sharp	Add a drop of antiseptic to warm water (boiled and allowed to cool), and bathe the cut gently. If it gets red and inflamed, **take your hamster to the vet**.

Length of life

A hamster can live to be one-and-a-half to two years old, occasionally a little more.

But, however well looked after, hamsters sometimes die while still young, perhaps from an illness or after an accidental fall. It is always upsetting when a pet dies, but especially if you do not know the cause. So, if your hamster dies and you do not know why, talk to your vet about it. He may be able to tell you what went wrong.

And, if you really enjoyed your hamster, do not be put off having another to take its place. But of course you will need to clean and disinfect the cage thoroughly, along with everything in it, to make sure no infection is passed on to your new hamster.

Hibernation

Wild hamsters hibernate in winter when food is even more scarce than usual in the desert.

Pet hamsters rarely do this, but should you find your hamster curled up very tight, hardly seeming to breathe, and it has been allowed to become colder than usual, do not try to rouse it. Just put the cage in a warmer place, and it should wake up naturally in a few hours.

Never touch or try to pick up a hamster when it is sleeping deeply. Even if it is not hibernating, being woken this way will frighten it.

Unexpected babies

Breeding hamsters is best left to the professional breeders, because expert handling is needed to choose the right time for mating, and to prevent the male from being attacked and hurt by the female.

Also there is the very real problem of finding good homes for the young – as many as ten or more can be born in one litter.

It is very unlikely, but it just might happen that you buy a female hamster which is already pregnant. Hamster babies are born sixteen days after mating.

You will know if your hamster does have some unexpected babies because you will hear their squeaks coming from the nest. **Do not disturb the nest to look at them**, or the mother may panic and attack them – her instinctive way of protecting them.

Hamsters are born quite helpless. They cannot see or hear, and they have no fur.

It is advisable to look for help on how to rear the babies in some of the books listed on page 31. Better still, consult your vet.

Begin at once to look for homes for the babies, because when they are only five weeks old they must be housed separately or they will begin to fight.

You can tell which sex a hamster is by looking at its hindquarters, which in a male (*above*) taper towards the tail, but in a female (*below*) end in a shallow curve.

Russian hamsters

Russian hamsters are 7 to 8 cm long, and can be recognized by the line of dark fur running from head to tail.

They are social animals, which in the wild live in family groups. So it is possible to keep more than one in the same cage.

If you want to keep Russian hamsters, you can follow the advice given for Golden hamsters apart from one or two points.

First, it is possible to keep more than one Russian hamster in the same cage without their quarrelling. Even so, watch them carefully. When the females are pregnant, they can sometimes attack and hurt the males, and need to be kept in a separate cage.

Secondly, as they are half the size of Golden hamsters make sure the bars of the cage are close enough, or they will escape.

Lastly, Russian hamsters need to be handled every day to stay tame, unlike Golden hamsters, which once tame, will always be tame.

All through its life, your hamster will depend on you for everything it needs. It will look to you for companionship as well as for its food, which it cannot go out and find for itself as it would if it was wild.

Your hamster will give you a lot of fun. In return, do your best to keep it healthy and happy and make its life as interesting as possible.

Further reading

Beginners Guide to Hamsters
Leila Watts
Paradise Press, 1991

Care For your Hamster
RSPCA Pet Guide
Collins, 1990

Hamsters
Susan Meredith
Osborne, 1999

Index